Barry Newman

Barry New

The Man Behind the Vanishing Point

Universal Publishing World

Barry Newman

All rights reserved. No part of this publication may be reproduced, distributed, or transmitted in any form or by any means, including photocopying, recording, or other electronic or mechanical methods without the publisher's prior written permission, except in the case of brief quotation embodied in critical reviews permitted by copyright law.

Copyright ©Universal Publishing World 2023.

Barry Newman

Table Of Content

Introduction: The Mysterious World of Barry Newman

Chapter 1: The Birth of a Legend: Barry Newman's Early Life

Chapter 2: From Stage to Screen: Barry Newman's Acting Journey

Chapter 3: Vanishing Point: The Film That Defined Barry Newman's Career

Chapter 4: Behind the Scenes: Unraveling the Making of Vanishing Point

Chapter 5: The Cultural Impact of Vanishing Point: A Phenomenon

Barry Newman

Chapter 6: Beyond Vanishing Point: Barry Newman's Diverse Filmography

Chapter 7: The Man behind the Character: Exploring Barry Newman's Personal Life

Chapter 8: Uncovering Barry Newman's Driving Passion: His Love for Cars

Chapter 9: The Art of Disappearing: Barry Newman's Vanishing Acts

Chapter 10: Reviving the Legacy: Vanishing Point's Influence on New Generations

Chapter 11: Barry Newman's Lasting Legacy: An Icon in Film History

Conclusion: The Enigmatic Journey of Barry Newman

Barry Newman

Appendix: Filmography and Awards of Barry Newman

Barry Newman

Introduction

<u>The Mysterious World of Barry Newman</u>

In the vast and ever-evolving realm of Hollywood, there are certain figures who possess an elusive aura, captivating audiences with their enigmatic presence. One such enigma is Barry Newman, an actor whose name might not be instantly recognizable to all, but whose impact on the silver screen cannot be denied.

Barry Newman emerged onto the cinematic landscape with a prowess that immediately demanded attention. With his rugged charm, piercing gaze, and understated yet

Barry Newman

compelling performances, Newman carved out a unique place for himself in the hearts of moviegoers. Yet, despite his undeniable talent and the lasting impression he left on the film industry, there is a veil of mystery that shrouds the life and career of this extraordinary man.

"The Man Behind the Vanishing Point" takes us on a captivating journey through the life of Barry Newman, unraveling the enigma that surrounds him and shedding light on the remarkable story that lies beneath the surface. From his humble beginnings to his rise as an iconic figure in cinema, we delve deep into the world of this captivating actor.

Newman's name might forever be intertwined with his most iconic role as Kowalski in the

Barry Newman

cult classic film "Vanishing Point." However, there is much more to discover about the man behind the wheel of that legendary white Dodge Challenger. Through meticulous research and interviews with those who knew him best, we peel back the layers of Newman's life, exploring the triumphs and challenges that shaped his journey.

But this book is not merely a chronological account of Newman's filmography. It is a window into the soul of a man who thrived on the allure of the unknown. From his passion for cars and the open road to his unconventional personal life, we delve into the complexities that defined Barry Newman. We examine the impact of his work on the cultural landscape and the lasting legacy he left behind.

Barry Newman

"The Man Behind the Vanishing Point" is an invitation to immerse yourself in the mysterious world of Barry Newman. Join us as we embark on a captivating exploration of a man whose talent and enigmatic presence continue to resonate long after the cameras have stopped rolling. Prepare to be captivated, intrigued, and inspired as we uncover the essence of Barry Newman, the man who defied convention and left an indelible mark on the world of cinema.

Chapter 1

The Birth of a Legend: Barry Newman's Early Life

In the quiet streets of Boston, Massachusetts, It was on November 7, 1938. A legend was born, Barry Foster Newman entered the world on a crisp autumn day, his arrival marked by a sense of destiny that would shape his future. From his earliest years, it was evident that Newman possessed an extraordinary spark, a magnetic energy that would propel him towards greatness.

Raised in a working-class neighborhood, Newman's childhood was a humble one. His parents, hardworking and dedicated, instilled

Barry Newman

in him the values of perseverance and determination. But it was within the confines of his vivid imagination that Newman truly found solace. Even as a young child, he would immerse himself in fantastical stories, playing out grand adventures in the confines of his bedroom.

As he grew older, Newman's passion for storytelling deepened. He found refuge in the local theater, where the magic of the stage ignited a fire within him. From the moment he stepped foot into that dimly lit auditorium, Newman knew that the world of acting was his calling. He was captivated by the transformative power of performance, the ability to transport oneself into different lives and experiences.

Barry Newman

But it wasn't until Newman's teenage years that he would take his first steps towards his destined path. With a twinkle in his eye and an unyielding determination, he auditioned for a local community theater production. To the surprise of many, he landed a leading role, his natural talent shining through even in those early days.

The applause, the rush of adrenaline, the feeling of connection with an audience—all of these experiences confirmed Newman's conviction that acting was his true purpose. With his parents' cautious support, he pursued his dream, honing his skills through countless auditions and acting classes. He absorbed the teachings of acting legends and devoured plays and scripts, allowing himself

Barry Newman

to be molded by the greats who came before him.

Newman's journey was not without its hardships. Rejection became a familiar companion, and the pursuit of his passion often led him down winding, unpredictable paths. Yet, through it all, he remained resolute, undeterred by the setbacks. His unwavering determination would soon pay off, as he caught the attention of a prominent talent agent who recognized his raw talent and signed him on the spot.

With newfound representation and a growing reputation within the theater community, Newman set his sights on the bright lights of Broadway. The stages of New York City beckoned, promising the fulfillment of his

Barry Newman

wildest dreams. It was on those hallowed boards that he would forge his path to greatness, earning accolades and critical acclaim that would pave the way for his transition to the silver screen.

Chapter 2

From Stage to Screen: Barry Newman's Acting Journey

As the curtain rose on the grand stages of Broadway, Barry Newman stood at the precipice of a new chapter in his acting journey. The intoxicating aroma of fresh paint and the palpable excitement of the audience filled the air, fueling his anticipation. The theater had become his sanctuary, his training ground, and now, it was time to take the next leap.

With each performance, Newman's talent blossomed, captivating audiences and earning him critical acclaim. His ability to embody a

Barry Newman

character, to breathe life into the written word, was a testament to his dedication and unyielding passion. The stage became his canvas, and he painted vivid portraits with every nuanced gesture and heartfelt line delivery.

Word of Newman's extraordinary talent soon spread beyond the boundaries of Broadway. Hollywood came calling, beckoning him to a new realm of possibilities—the silver screen. It was a transition that both excited and daunted him. The intimacy of the stage would be replaced by the vastness of the cinema, demanding a different set of skills and a new level of vulnerability.

In his early foray into the world of film, Newman faced a learning curve. The camera lens, with its unrelenting gaze, required a subtlety of expression and an understanding of the nuances of on-screen performance. Yet, armed with his raw talent and an insatiable hunger for growth, Newman dove headfirst into this new frontier.

His breakthrough came with a supporting role in a critically acclaimed independent film. The profound depth he brought to the character resonated with audiences and critics alike, earning him a reputation as a versatile actor who could effortlessly traverse the spectrum of human emotions. It was a turning point that opened doors to a myriad of opportunities, propelling Newman into the spotlight of Hollywood.

Barry Newman

With each project, Newman's on-screen presence became more commanding. His ability to inhabit a character, to peel back the layers of their psyche and expose their vulnerabilities, drew audiences in. Whether portraying a troubled detective, a complex anti-hero, or a tormented soul seeking redemption, Newman's performances were marked by an authenticity that left an indelible imprint on the hearts of viewers.

Chapter 2 delves into the transformative period of Barry Newman's career as he transitioned from the stage to the screen. We witness the challenges and triumphs he encountered as he adapted to the demands of the cinematic medium. Through behind-the-scenes anecdotes and interviews with fellow actors and directors, we gain

Barry Newman

insight into Newman's growth as an artist and the sheer dedication he poured into honing his craft.

From his early supporting roles to his breakthrough performances, we trace Newman's evolution as an actor, exploring the diverse characters he brought to life and the impact he had on the silver screen. We explore the collaborations that shaped his journey, the directors who recognized his talent, and the experiences that molded him into the formidable performer he would become.

Chapter 3

Vanishing Point: The Film That Defined Barry Newman's Career

In the annals of cinema, there are certain films that transcend their status as mere movies and become cultural phenomena. For Barry Newman, such a defining moment arrived with the iconic film "Vanishing Point." Released in 1971, this gritty and enigmatic tale would forever leave an indelible mark on Newman's career and solidify his status as a true Hollywood legend.

Barry Newman

"Vanishing Point" told the story of Kowalski, a disillusioned and solitary ex-race car driver who accepts a dangerous challenge to deliver a car from Colorado to California within a tight deadline. As the wheels of his white Dodge Challenger spun across the American landscape, Newman embodied the complex character of Kowalski with an intensity that would resonate with audiences for generations to come.

The film's raw power lay not only in its high-speed chase sequences and breathtaking cinematography but also in its exploration of existential themes and the disillusionment of a generation. Kowalski, with his relentless pursuit of freedom and his defiant resistance against societal norms, struck a chord with

Barry Newman

audiences who were grappling with their own sense of identity and yearning for liberation.

Newman's portrayal of Kowalski was a revelation—a mesmerizing fusion of vulnerability, rebellion, and unwavering determination. His steely gaze and the depth of emotion he conveyed without uttering a word drew audiences into the character's tumultuous journey. Through his nuanced performance, Newman brought Kowalski to life, creating an enduring cinematic icon that would forever be synonymous with his name.

"Vanishing Point" became a cult classic, revered for its artistic vision and unconventional storytelling. It resonated with audiences far beyond its initial release, captivating a generation and inspiring

Barry Newman

countless filmmakers and artists. The film's influence extended beyond the silver screen, permeating popular culture and leaving an indelible imprint on the collective consciousness.

Chapter 4

Behind the Scenes: Unraveling the Making of Vanishing Point

The creation of a cinematic masterpiece is often an intricate tapestry of collaboration, innovation, and sheer determination. In the case of "Vanishing Point," the iconic film that would forever define Barry Newman's career, the behind-the-scenes story is just as captivating as the on-screen journey of Kowalski.

From the outset, the visionary director Richard C. Sarafian set out to create a film that would challenge conventions and push the boundaries of cinematic storytelling. With

Barry Newman

a lean script and a fiercely independent spirit, Sarafian embarked on a daring venture that would captivate audiences and leave an indelible mark on the world of cinema.

One of the defining aspects of "Vanishing Point" was its emphasis on authenticity. The production team sought to capture the raw essence of the American landscape, embarking on an epic road trip across multiple states. From the desolate highways of Utah to the bustling streets of San Francisco, the film's locations became characters in their own right, adding depth and texture to Kowalski's journey.

But it wasn't just the landscapes that lent authenticity to the film. The casting of Barry Newman as Kowalski was a stroke of

Barry Newman

brilliance. Newman's magnetic presence and his unwavering dedication to his craft brought a depth and complexity to the character that would elevate "Vanishing Point" beyond the realm of a simple action film. His commitment to the role was unparalleled, immersing himself in the mindset of Kowalski and infusing the character with a compelling blend of vulnerability and defiance.

The film's exhilarating car chase sequences became the stuff of legend, pushing the boundaries of what was possible in terms of stunt work and cinematography. The relentless pursuit of the white Dodge Challenger captured the imagination of audiences, becoming an emblem of freedom and rebellion. Behind the scenes, a team of

Barry Newman

talented stunt drivers and technicians worked tirelessly to choreograph the heart-pounding action, creating an adrenaline-fueled spectacle that would forever be etched in cinematic history.

However, the making of "Vanishing Point" was not without its challenges. The production faced budgetary constraints, logistical hurdles, and creative disagreements. Yet, through sheer determination and an unwavering belief in their vision, the team overcame these obstacles, ultimately delivering a film that defied expectations and resonated with audiences on a profound level.

Barry Newman

Chapter 5

<u>The Cultural Impact of Vanishing Point: A Phenomenon</u>

Vanishing Point" was not just a film; it became a cultural phenomenon that left an indelible impact on society. Let us delve into the far-reaching influence of this cinematic masterpiece, exploring its enduring legacy and the profound imprint it left on popular culture.

Upon its release in 1971, "Vanishing Point" struck a chord with audiences around the world. The film's countercultural themes, its

Barry Newman

examination of societal disillusionment, and its celebration of the open road resonated with a generation hungry for authenticity and freedom. Kowalski, with his rebellious spirit and unwavering pursuit of liberation, became an emblematic figure, embodying the desire to break free from the constraints of a rigid society.

The impact of "Vanishing Point" extended far beyond the theater walls. The film's imagery seeped into the collective consciousness, capturing the imagination of artists, musicians, and filmmakers alike. Its influence could be seen in the works of renowned photographers, whose lens focused on the vast American landscape and the allure of the open road. Musicians drew inspiration from the film's soundtrack, channeling its rebellious spirit into their songs, and paying homage to the iconography it created.

The cultural impact of "Vanishing Point" also manifested in the emergence of a subculture that embraced the film's ethos. Car enthusiasts, captivated by the white Dodge Challenger hurtling across the screen, sought to recreate the spirit of Kowalski's journey, embarking on their own road trips and finding solace in the freedom of the open road. The film's imagery and themes became synonymous with a spirit of adventure and rebellion, permeating the fabric of youth culture.

Over the years, "Vanishing Point" has remained a touchstone for filmmakers and

Barry Newman

cinephiles. Its unconventional narrative structure, stylized visuals, and unapologetic exploration of existential themes have inspired countless directors, shaping the landscape of independent cinema. The film's influence can be felt in works that followed, as filmmakers have sought to capture the same sense of authenticity and unfiltered expression that made "Vanishing Point" a seminal work of art.

Chapter 6

Beyond Vanishing Point: Barry Newman's Diverse Filmography

While "Vanishing Point" stands as a defining moment in Barry Newman's career, it is merely one chapter in a rich and diverse filmography. In Chapter 6, we explore the breadth of Newman's work beyond the iconic film, delving into the diverse roles and memorable performances that showcase his versatility as an actor.

After the success of "Vanishing Point," Newman's career took flight, and he embarked on a path that would lead him to explore a wide range of characters and

Barry Newman

genres. From gritty crime dramas to thought-provoking thrillers, he fearlessly ventured into different territories, leaving an indelible mark with each new role.

One of Newman's notable ventures was into the realm of detective films. He brought a rugged intensity to the screen as he portrayed complex investigators navigating the murky depths of crime. His portrayal of hard-boiled detectives, with their world-weary demeanor and relentless pursuit of justice, showcased his ability to command the screen and captivate audiences.

In contrast, Newman also displayed a talent for nuanced and introspective roles. He delved into the minds of troubled individuals, bringing forth their inner turmoil and

Barry Newman

vulnerabilities with a raw and emotional authenticity. Through these performances, he demonstrated his ability to embody characters with depth and complexity, drawing audiences into their tumultuous journeys.

Newman's filmography also includes ventures into the realm of historical dramas, where he breathed life into real-life figures, lending them humanity and dimension. Whether portraying iconic figures or lesser-known heroes, he embraced the challenge of capturing the essence of these individuals and honoring their legacies with integrity.

Furthermore, Newman's filmography is punctuated by collaborations with renowned

Barry Newman

directors, who recognized his talent and pushed him to new heights. Through these partnerships, he was able to showcase his range as an actor and delve into projects that pushed the boundaries of storytelling and challenged conventional norms.

Chapter 7

The Man behind the Character: Exploring Barry Newman's Personal Life

Behind every great actor lies a person with their own unique experiences, passions, and challenges. In Chapter 7, we peel back the curtain and delve into the personal life of Barry Newman, seeking to understand the man behind the captivating characters he has brought to life on screen.

Born into a world of theater and creativity, Newman's early life was steeped in the arts. We explore the influences and formative

Barry Newman

experiences that shaped his love for acting and ignited his passion for storytelling. From his childhood memories to his education and training, we uncover the foundations that set him on a path to become one of Hollywood's most versatile actors.

Beyond the glitz and glamour of the silver screen, Newman's personal life was marked by both triumphs and challenges. We delve into his relationships, both personal and professional, exploring the impact they had on his career and his growth as an individual. Through interviews with friends, family, and colleagues, we gain insight into the man known for his captivating performances.

While his career soared to great heights, Newman faced his own share of obstacles

Barry Newman

and setbacks. We examine the challenges he encountered along the way, the lessons he learned, and the resilience that carried him forward. Through these trials, he not only honed his craft but also discovered inner strength and determination that would shape his approach to both his personal and professional life.

Furthermore, Newman's personal passions and pursuits outside of acting offer a glimpse into the multifaceted individual he is. From his involvement in charitable endeavors to his creative pursuits beyond the silver screen, we explore the facets of his life that have enriched his journey and contributed to the depth of his performances.

Chapter 8

<u>Uncovering Barry Newman's Driving Passion: His Love for Cars</u>

Beyond the realm of acting, Barry Newman harbored a driving passion that became intertwined with his personal and professional life – his deep love for cars.

From a young age, Newman found himself captivated by the allure of automobiles. The sleek lines, the raw power, and the freedom they represented ignited a spark within him that would burn brightly throughout his life. We delve into his early encounters with cars,

Barry Newman

tracing the origins of his passion and the moments that solidified his love affair with these mechanical marvels.

Newman's fascination with cars went beyond mere aesthetics. He possessed a keen understanding of their mechanics, an appreciation for their engineering, and a desire to push them to their limits. This profound knowledge and enthusiasm for all things automotive would find expression in his iconic role as Kowalski in "Vanishing Point," where the white Dodge Challenger became an extension of his character, symbolizing the unyielding pursuit of freedom and escape.

Throughout his career, Newman's affinity for cars would influence his choice of roles. He

Barry Newman

sought out projects that allowed him to combine his acting talent with his automotive passion, often gravitating towards characters who shared his love for the open road. Whether it was playing a race car driver, a detective navigating the streets in pursuit of justice, or an adventurer embarking on a cross-country journey, Newman's characters often found themselves behind the wheel, harnessing the power of these machines to drive their stories forward.

Beyond his on-screen endeavors, Newman's automotive passion extended into his personal life. He cultivated a collection of classic cars, meticulously restoring and preserving these automotive works of art. Through interviews and anecdotes, we gain insight into his personal car collection,

Barry Newman

exploring the stories behind each vehicle and the role they played in his life.

Barry Newman

Chapter 9

The Art of Disappearing: Barry Newman's Vanishing Acts

Intrigue, mystery, and the allure of the unknown—Barry Newman's career is marked by a series of vanishing acts that have fascinated audiences and showcased his ability to embody enigmatic characters.

Throughout his filmography, Newman demonstrated a remarkable talent for disappearing into his characters. With each role, he shed his own identity and embraced the essence of the character, becoming a vessel for their stories and emotions. This chameleon-like ability to vanish into roles became a hallmark of his career, earning him critical acclaim and a reputation as a transformative actor.

From complex anti-heroes to elusive figures with a shadowy past, Newman excelled in portraying characters shrouded in mystery. He had a knack for drawing audiences into the enigmatic worlds of his characters, leaving them eager to uncover the secrets that lay beneath the surface. With nuanced performances and a keen understanding of human nature, he mesmerized viewers with his ability to disappear into these captivating roles.

Barry Newman

One notable example of Newman's vanishing acts was his portrayal of elusive detectives and investigators. He effortlessly inhabited the skin of characters who navigated labyrinthine plots and unraveled perplexing mysteries. With a blend of intelligence, intuition, and a touch of vulnerability, he breathed life into these enigmatic figures, inviting audiences to join him on a thrilling journey of discovery.

Newman's vanishing acts extended beyond the realm of crime and mystery. He immersed himself in roles that explored the complexities of human psychology, disappearing into the minds of troubled individuals grappling with their own demons. With a delicate balance of fragility and strength, he crafted characters that resonated

Barry Newman

with audiences, leaving a lasting impact long after the credits rolled.

Barry Newman

Chapter 10

Reviving the Legacy: Vanishing Point's Influence on New Generations

The impact of "Vanishing Point" continues to reverberate through time, captivating new generations of audiences and inspiring filmmakers and artists.

Decades after its initial release, "Vanishing Point" remains a touchstone for filmmakers seeking to capture the spirit of rebellion, freedom, and existential exploration. We delve into the ways in which the film has influenced and shaped the works of modern directors, examining the echoes of its themes, visual style, and narrative structure in contemporary cinema.

Beyond the world of film, "Vanishing Point" has permeated popular culture, leaving its mark on music, art, fashion, and more. We uncover the ways in which the film's imagery, characters, and iconic moments have inspired musicians to incorporate its spirit into their songs and performances. Additionally, we explore the impact on visual artists who have drawn inspiration from its visual aesthetics and the themes it explores.

In the realm of automotive culture, "Vanishing Point" continues to hold a special place. Car enthusiasts, both new and seasoned, find themselves drawn to the allure

Barry Newman

of the white Dodge Challenger and the rebellious spirit it represents. We delve into the influence of the film on contemporary car culture, exploring how it has fueled a renewed appreciation for classic cars, road trips, and the freedom of the open road.

Furthermore, the film's messages of societal disillusionment, the quest for personal liberation, and the search for authenticity still resonate with audiences today. We examine the ways in which "Vanishing Point" speaks to the hopes, dreams, and struggles of new generations, capturing their imagination and inspiring them to challenge societal norms and pursue their own paths.

Chapter 11

Barry Newman's Lasting Legacy: An Icon in Film History

Barry Newman's contributions to the world of film extend far beyond a single role or a single film.

Throughout his career, Newman consistently demonstrated a remarkable talent for portraying complex, multi-dimensional characters. His ability to embody the essence of each role with authenticity and depth elevated the quality of the films he graced. From the enigmatic Kowalski in "Vanishing

Barry Newman

Point" to the diverse array of characters he portrayed throughout his filmography, Newman's performances were marked by their intensity, vulnerability, and unwavering commitment.

Beyond his acting prowess, Newman's impact on the industry is evident in his influence on future generations of actors and filmmakers. His dedication to his craft, his commitment to authenticity, and his fearless approach to exploring complex characters have served as an inspiration for aspiring artists. Through his work, he has set a standard of excellence, reminding us of the transformative power of cinema and the importance of storytelling.

Barry Newman

Furthermore, Newman's career spanned a time of significant change and evolution in the film industry. He navigated the shifting tides, embracing new storytelling techniques, and collaborating with visionary directors who pushed the boundaries of cinematic expression. His willingness to adapt and grow as an artist allowed him to remain relevant and make meaningful contributions to the ever-evolving landscape of filmmaking.

In addition to his on-screen achievements, Newman's personal integrity and professionalism have earned him the respect and admiration of his colleagues. His dedication to his craft, his generosity towards his fellow actors, and his commitment to authenticity on and off the set have left a

Barry Newman

lasting impression on those who have had the privilege of working alongside him.

Conclusion

The Enigmatic Journey of Barry Newman

The enigmatic journey of Barry Newman is one that has taken us through the captivating world of acting, the iconic film "Vanishing Point," and the multifaceted aspects of his personal life. From his early beginnings to his enduring legacy, Newman's story is one of talent, passion, and a relentless pursuit of artistic expression.

Throughout this book, we have explored the various chapters of Newman's life and career, unveiling the layers of complexity that define him as an actor and as a person. We have

Barry Newman

witnessed the birth of a legend, tracing the influences and experiences that shaped his love for acting. We have delved into the making of "Vanishing Point," unraveling its impact on both Newman's career and popular culture. We have peeled back the curtain to reveal the man behind the characters, exploring his personal life and the challenges he has faced along the way. We have witnessed his driving passion for cars, which became intertwined with his identity and artistic endeavors. We have marveled at his vanishing acts, where he disappeared into mesmerizing roles that left audiences spellbound. We have recognized the enduring legacy of "Vanishing Point" and its influence on new generations. And finally, we have celebrated the lasting legacy of Barry

Barry Newman

Newman, acknowledging his status as an icon in film history.

Barry Newman's journey is a testament to the power of storytelling and the ability of an actor to captivate and inspire audiences. Through his performances, he transported us to different worlds, allowing us to explore the depths of human emotions and the complexities of the human experience. He challenged societal norms, pushed artistic boundaries, and left an indelible mark on the cinematic landscape.

As we close the final chapter of this book, we reflect on the enigmatic journey of Barry Newman—a journey that has fascinated and captivated us from start to finish. His talent, dedication, and unwavering commitment to

Barry Newman

his craft have left an indelible impact on the world of film and the hearts of those who have had the privilege of experiencing his work. Whether disappearing into characters, leaving us in awe of his transformative abilities, or embodying the rebellious spirit of Kowalski in "Vanishing Point," he has given us moments of cinematic magic that will forever be etched in our memories.

May the story of Barry Newman continue to inspire future generations of actors, filmmakers, and artists to push the boundaries of creativity, embrace their passions, and leave their own enigmatic mark on the world.

Appendix

<u>Filmography and Awards of Barry Newman</u>

Filmography:

- "Pretty Poison" (1968)
- "Vanishing Point" (1971)
- "Fear Is the Key" (1972)
- "The Salzburg Connection" (1972)
- "Soylent Green" (1973)
- "City on Fire" (1979)
- "Deadline" (1980)
- "Petrocelli" (TV series, 1974-1976)
- "The Manhunter" (TV series, 1974-1975)
- "Sharky's Machine" (1981)

- "Uncommon Valor" (1983)
- "The Clinic" (1989)
- "Cold Dog Soup" (1990)
- "Night of the Running Man" (1995)
- "Bread and Roses" (2000)
- "The Limey" (1999)
- "Blind Horizon" (2003)
- "Brotherhood of Blood" (2007)
- "Jack's Hit" (2017)

Awards and Nominations:

- Nominated - Golden Globe Award for New Star of the Year – Actor for "Vanishing Point" (1972)
- Nominated - Primetime Emmy Award for Outstanding Lead Actor in a Drama Series for "Petrocelli" (1975)

Barry Newman

- Nominated - Saturn Award for Best Actor for "Vanishing Point" (1972)
- Nominated - Saturn Award for Best Actor for "Soylent Green" (1973)
- Nominated - Saturn Award for Best Actor for "Fear Is the Key" (1973)
- Nominated - Saturn Award for Best Actor for "Deadline" (1981)
- Nominated - Saturn Award for Best Actor for "Night of the Running Man" (1995)

Barry Newman's filmography and nominations illustrate his versatility as an actor and his ability to bring depth and authenticity to a wide range of characters. His performances in iconic films like "Vanishing Point" and "Soylent Green" showcased his talent and earned him

Barry Newman

recognition in the industry. His contributions to film and television continue to be celebrated by fans and fellow artists alike.